GW00578128

THE ART
OF
LONG NETTING

HAROLD WYMAN

COCH-Y-BONDDU BOOKS

ACKNOWLEDGEMENTS

I dedicate this work to my son Arthur, without whose inspiration and practical help this book would not have been written.

My most sincere thanks go to Captain D.F.Myddelton of Chirk Castle Estate who allowed us to use his land for the photography; to Mr Tony Butler, Pastor of Oswestry Community Church for taking most of the photographs and for the use of his well-trained German pointer; and to Barbara and Troy Wyman for their invaluable assistance.

First published in 1989 by Dickson Price Publishers.
Reprinted 1997 by Coch-y-Bonddu Books.
All rights reserved.

ISBN 0 9528510 3 2

Published and distributed by
COCH-Y-BONDDU BOOKS
Machynlleth, Powys, SY20 8DJ.
Tel 01654 702837   Fax 01654 702857

Printed and bound in Great Britain by
Redwood Books, Trowbridge, Wiltshire

CONTENTS

Introduction

I LEARNED THE LONG netting art from a man called Thomas Moor and a better teacher I could not have wished for. I will introduce you to this remarkable character.

I had heard many tales about Thomas before making his acquaintance. His personal appearance did not give the lie to the stories. It was a year or so before the second world war in the pre-myxomatosis era when rabbits had reached plague proportions and I was with a friend, Pat Burke, in the Royal Oak on the town's high street, when a man entered, took the room in with a glance and moved to the bar. 'Who is he, Pat?' I asked. 'Come on, I will introduce you.' 'Harold, this is the famous Wrexham poacher, Thomas Moor.' This man, I had learned, was regarded by all who knew him as a master of the nocturnal art. One glance convinced me that he was an extremely determined character and he looked as if he had just stepped out of the pages of a book into real life.

A well-worn dark blue pin-stripe suit, the waistcoat sporting a fine watch chain, silk neckerchief and cloth cap cocked on one side, made up his raiment. His height no more than five feet six, a weather-beaten face with a long thin nose and eyes as blue as the sky. Add to this the wide brows and high cheek bones of the fighting man and one may form a picture of this remarkable man. During the evening I narrated a youthful exploit that appeared to appeal to his rugged nature and this was the start of a life-long friendship. The first surprise I received was when he informed me that he was no longer a poacher but a free lance rabbit-catcher. The explosion of the rabbit population and resultant damage which ensued, caused the owners of a number of estates to overlook his former activities and gladly accept his offer of controlling the rabbit population. In one season's long netting over a large area of Shropshire, Thomas Moor and I killed over four thousand rabbits and remember, others fared equally well. In the pre myxomatosis era, Shropshire was the Wrexham long netters' paradise.

Thomas, I came to realise, was not just a master of his craft, but a person of considerable intelligence. An avid reader and of strongly held political opinions; I was present on one occasion when he defended his political views with great gusto and wit. Strangely enough, for all his reputation as an ex-poacher, I found him to be a person of high integrity and the legality, or otherwise, of taking rabbits without permission I am sure never entered his head, though both his parents who were members of the Salvation Army, took a dim view of his youthful activities.

Thomas and his peers were not the type one finds portrayed in most poaching books. The now traditional image given is of a man born in the country, living in a tied cottage owned by the squire from whom he poached fur and feather. These men did exist, but I know from personal experience and information imparted by Thomas Moor that the real dare-devil poachers were bred, reared and slaved in the rough, tough environment of the early industrial areas. It was in the industrial communities, such as the mining areas around Wrexham, South Wales and elsewhere where life was unbelievably hard, that many brave and bold men evolved. Products of history and the unyielding harshness of their environment, they were not cowardly as portrayed in the old-type poaching novel.

The late-Victorian industrial era produced many such as Thomas Moor; poachers they certainly were but they also possessed great bravery and fortitude, serving the nation courageously on many a far-flung battle field, often sacrificing their lives in a desperate forlorn action, and what for? In many an instance to preserve the vested interests of the rich land-owning gentry who sat as magistrates and sent to prison these very same men who fought, as did Thomas Moor and many of his contemporaries, with distinction.

There have been marked changes in the country scene around me as the decades have passed. Many of the tall hawthorn hedges where the song birds abounded, have been grubbed out and with them have gone the ancient rabbit warrens, the rabbit population has also been greatly reduced by the introduction of myxomatosis. The copses in sheltered hollows that gave roosting for the wandering cock pheasants are fast disappearing, but thankfully many large pheasant coverts still abound and the syndicate pheasant shooting sportsman should in part be thanked for this. The season's payment made to the estates in order to enjoy their sporting activity, has no doubt saved many a woodland from destruction. In most of these, along with the reared birds, rabbits, badgers and a variety of wild life also find refuge. Long may it be so.

I hope the information in this book will give the professional and amateur long netter a comprehensive and accurate picture of all aspects of the art of long netting, an art that has been practised in one form or another for centuries, and no doubt will continue to be so for as long as there are rabbits to catch.

—1—

The Quarry

T HE RABBIT, ACCORDING TO the historians, was introduced to these isles following the Norman Conquest. No liberty of movement was given and they were confined to selected areas, known as 'warrens'. These defined areas were jealously guarded by rabbit keepers, or warreners, who worked them for the profit received from the sale of fur and flesh. The early warrens were open, but were later enclosed. It became inevitable that as time passed a number of the bolder element of the rabbit population escaped the enclosed confines of the areas and established wild breeding colonies. It was, in fact, due to these large wild breeding colonies producing just as efficiently and at no cost, that the private enclosures were abandoned. The early eighteen hundreds saw the demise of the now unprofitable enclosed areas and by the mid eighteen hundreds the wild population was exploding. The result was, that by the dawn of the twentieth century the wild rabbit was at plague proportions.

To see a field brown over with feeding rabbits was a common sight when I was a child and young man. On entering the fields of a summer's evening I delighted at the spectacle as they swarmed toward the sanctuary of the wood. Many of the saplings along the woodland caught the eye, standing dead, bleached white round the base where the rabbits had ringed them by stripping the bark to a height of about two feet. One such woodland comes readily to mind, covering an area large enough to allow the long netter to drop his nets on nine separate sets. The first season Thomas Moor and I worked them at the owner's behest. He was delighted when at the end of the season our tally was close to three thousand killed. Despite the depredation of that first season, those nine sets yielded regular seasonal catches of between fifteen hundred to two thousand, until the advent of the dreaded myxomatosis.

The reproductive potential of the rabbit is amazing. The close of a season finds them drastically reduced, yet each new season sees them well replenished and present in good numbers. It has been stated that the doe gives birth to seven to nine kits. This premise is debatable, for whenever a doe in young has been taken by me in January or February, four or five young was the norm, seven was an exception. Whether the doe carried this number of young because of the early months and later, as the season advanced, produced larger litters, I am not qualified to speculate upon, for I ceased operations at the first signs of milky does in the nets. This can be as early as late January if the weather is mild, or as late as March depending on the whim of the elements. A rabbit possibly reproduces herself twenty times during a breeding season and some times more.

Myxomatosis is a vile disease, laboratory manufactured and first used in the early nineteen fifties, which decimated the rabbit population by ninety-nine per cent. The sight of fields covered with dead and dying rabbits was heart rending.

Following the first outbreak I noticed the improvements in the grass and shrubs in many areas. No longer the common sight of the cornfields bordering the coverts scythed by the feeding rabbits to a distance of some thirty or forty feet into the field; from the farmer's point of view a welcome phenomenon. The one per cent that survived this first and most devastatingly effective attack by the disease bred as only the rabbit can and by nineteen sixty I was again taking forty to fifty for a night's work. Despite further distribution of the disease, the rabbit made headway and by the nineteen seventies had made a remarkable recovery. The farmer is once again calling the long netter back into the fray against his dauntless foe, and as the long net

12

presents no danger of injury to livestock, it is in my opinion the most effective and humane method of controlling the rabbit population.

—2—

The Long Net

O N THE FIRST OCCASION that I called on Thomas Moor, his wife answered the door and ushered me into the parlour. It was close to eventide and the sole means of illumination was a single candle. Thomas was sitting near the bay window in order to take advantage of the fading light and knitting a long net which was practically completed. Part of the net hung from a hook screwed into the side of the window. He was working with amazing speed and dexterity. Rows of diamond meshes were being formed on a bone mesh board, the net-making needle was also of the same material. He had acquired these two articles of net-making equipment as a boy of twelve, I was subsequently told. He explained that his intention was to produce a fifty-yard net, twelve meshes deep, each mesh being two and a quarter inches from knot to knot, or as some measure, four and a half inches fully stretched on the diamond. The fifty yards entailed the making of one hundred yards of net, then spreading it between two lines. The traditional material of the Wrexham long netter was being used, twelve patent hemp.

Observing Thomas practising his net-making skills was fascinating; I resolved to learn this art and when I asked to be taught he was only too pleased to oblige. Removing the net from the hook he proceeded to teach me the knots required to form the diamond-shaped meshes, spending close to two hours painstakingly explaining and demonstrating. It was time well spent, for by the time I left his abode, I had been initiated into the long net-makers' art. I also learned the best way to dye a net. My companion insisted that to obtain a good killing colour, that is a colour that enables one to kill rabbits, even on a night of white clouds, was by dyeing the net brown, then running a dark green dye over the brown. This blend turned the net into a dark khaki which was the local netters' favourite colour.

I was six weeks making my first two long nets, under the supervision of Thomas. I also accepted his advice and dyed one dark and the other a lighter shade of khaki. Then both were lined with cotton runners. Next I visited the local blacksmith and ordered two pairs of anchor pins with the strict instruction that the join of each pin should be brazed in order to prevent the meshing being caught up in the ring of the anchor. Later I realised the value of the advice when out with a young long netter when Thomas was indisposed. The rings of his anchors not being completely closed, allowed the mesh to slip between the gap and his nets were virtually unusable that night.

The long netter of yesteryear's nets were very different from the modern shop-bought ones that are commonly in use today, made with nylon. The depth of the modern net I am sure would be considered much too deep and the four inch mesh fully stretched on the diamond would be considered too small. In my opinion this small mesh is the reason why many of the full-grown rabbits striking, bounce off and running back to the field, squat. They then become net shy. Neither would the old long netter entertain the thought of using a net containing only seventy-five yards of netting threaded onto two fifty-yard lines, because they lack running kill.

The following method is the one used by the Wrexham long netter of fifty years ago and still holds good today. Including the type of hemp favoured, and the size of mesh found most appropriate, the depth of the net was considered to be of the utmost importance; too deep and the net would be underfoot, interfering with the smooth working of the pegger; not enough depth was even worse, because of the lack of kill.

THE TRADITIONAL HEMP LONG NET

As already stated, the material most favoured in order to construct a strong yet light net, one that would lift and billow in the lightest breeze was twelve patent hemp. The diamond shaped meshes were formed from two strands of this fine hemp; the size of the mesh was a choice of two. A few of the lads, myself included, favoured the mesh size four and quarter inches when fully stretched out on the diamond. This size enabled us to catch the half-grown as well as the full-grown rabbits.

However, many of the old-timers who used the nets, long before my initiation, would never use a long net containing a mesh size less than four and a half inches when fully stretched on the diamond and twelve meshes deep. A fifty-yard net should, in their opinion, contain one hundred yards of netting threaded on to two fifty-yard lines. I agree with many of the views held by these men regarding the depth of the net and the size of the mesh. Albert Lovell, who is now a very old man, well over ninety years in fact, constructed his nets to the same design as his forbears. He explained that the full mesh net would allow the rabbit to slide its head through with ease, but was able to hold the creature if it tried to withdraw. Holding it firmly behind the ears. Old Albert believed any mesh smaller than full size would cause a number of adult rabbits to bounce off.

I commenced long netting invariably in mid-August, therefore a slightly smaller mesh was required in order to hold the half-grown rabbits and because my mesh was smaller, the net was made two mesh deeper, which meant the nets were fourteen deep instead of twelve. Long netting occasionally poses its problems, especially if one happens to be a professional warrener, because there are times when it is necessary, due to infestation of an estate with quarter- and half-grown rabbits, to reduce their numbers by July. The nylon net will account for a small proportion, but most will squeeze through and those held will be through and barely held by the haunches. A three-inch mesh is required to take the quarter-grown.

NYLON LONG NETS

Most young men taking up long netting today will probably opt

The author holding in his left hand a six-Z nylon long net and in his right a standard three-Z net (David Bishop).

for the nylon because they are the cheapest; these popular nets are available in a variety of lengths with a slight variation in depth from one manufacturer to another. Being constructed of varying thicknesses will of course have a bearing on their weight and this is a most important factor to consider when contemplating the purchase of one, or more. Without doubt the most popular of these nylon nets is the standard version. Three- or four-Z nylon runs the entire length of these nets, but there is a series of half meshes consisting of six-Z nylon both top and bottom through which the head and foot lines are threaded. These double-strength half mesh are a great advantage giving increased strength to the area where there is constant wear and tear caused by friction of the net running the lines when end setting. There is also the added strength when struck by a lot of rabbits.

The four-inch mesh of which all nylon nets consist would be much too small for the construction of a good killing hemp net, because the nature of nylon is such that it stretches. I understand the manufacturers' reasons for the introduction of the four-inch mesh, for I find on forcing my hand into these meshes that they stretch a quarter of an inch, equalling that of a full mesh hemp net. I obtained three of these standard nylon nets and having made what I considered to be necessary modifications, they have become very efficient rabbit killers, especially on wet nights, as they do not hold the water as long as hemp.

In order to ensure that these nets met my requirements I extended the seventy-five yards of netting because it was threaded on to two fifty-yard lines. This amounted to half a yard of kill, or slack net, to a yard of line. I knitted into each net an extra twenty-five yards. If one does not wish this addition, the only alternative is to reduce the length of the lines from fifty to forty yards. They are then, in my opinion, an excellent killing net.

The Six-Z Nylon Long net

Apart from the standard nylon I also possess two six-Z nylon nets, and, because of the previously mentioned problem, reduced them from fifty to forty yards and found they performed satisfactorily, albeit a little cumbersome compared to the standard version, especially when wet. Opinion has it that six-Z is stronger and less susceptible to breaks than the standard net.

Preference is also shown because the quarry is removed from the mesh more conveniently after being despatched. The first point is irrefutable, but the second will not stand investigation. The old timers did not refer to their nets as webs for nothing. They knew the importance of constructing them as fine and strong as possible in order that, on contact, they would cling to the body of the prey, rolling up and immobilizing them instantly. Tied in this manner the rabbit will naturally take longer to unravel; on the other hand one does not encounter the problem of rabbits bouncing off. The unthinking critic should ponder this point – the rabbit that is not securely enmeshed has a far greater chance of escape than the one that is.

On the first occasion that I worked six-Z nets, they were accompanied by two standard size. The night in question was wet and we set the nets on a place known as the 'Deer Sheds'. Returning from the beat we found a good catch in the nets, but quite a number contained by the six-Z were held by the head only, whereas all those held in the standard size were well enmeshed. Nevertheless, what suits one may be anathema to another. The nylon long net is here to stay and when constructed in the fashion I have described is a most useful addition to the long netter's equipment.

THE PRE-SET DROP NET

A brief description of this net and its function should suffice, as I am not sure whether there are sufficient practitioners to make it worthwhile describing in greater detail.

In order to hoist the net to a height that leaves the foot line four feet or so from the ground, a number of seven-foot lengths of three-quarter inch steel piping is required. These steel lofting poles are secured into the ground in a vertical position at regular intervals along the woodside. A separate slide bar thirty inches in length, with a ring welded top and bottom so that it will slide over the steel poles is essential.

The net is run out and secured to a small bobbin which is

fitted to the top and bottom of each thirty-inch slide bar. The net is then raised from the ground a section at a time. Each section is supported by a short steel pin which is inserted into a hole that has been drilled through each lofting pole. Thus, the whole net is held aloft by the short steel release pins. A line or length of cord is then fitted to the release pins along the entire system and an extra fifty yards ensures the dropping of the net from a distance whenever the operator is satisfied that enough bunnies have passed under the web.

Having read about the net being most effective in carrying out the purpose for which it was designed, my son Arthur and I decided to put it to the test. Approaching his friend David Bishop, Arthur asked him to make the equipment to the required measurements and within a couple of weeks Dave duly obliged. Each piece of equipment was perfectly made, from the steel uprights and slide bars to the release pins. Taking the net and equipment to a nearby field, Arthur and I lofted the net on to the poles. When fully set up, the line, or cord was pulled releasing the pins and the net dropped instantly. We were well pleased with the mechanics of what we like to call the Mansbridge-style drop net.

One Sunday evening in mid-July we decided to give this net its first serious trial. That first effort turned into a total disaster. Arriving at the estate where our job is to control the rabbit population, we discovered one field in particular was swarming with quarter- and half-grown bunnies. These, upon sighting us, went crashing into the undergrowth that ran along the edge of the wood. Our pre-set net was erected and the release cord trailed to cover a distance of seventy yards or more. We then vacated the scene of operation. Returning after an interval of two hours, we peered through the cover at the lofted net expecting to see the field covered with grazing rabbits. To our surprise, not one had ventured under the net. Leaving the scene of our disappointment and intent on returning well after dark, we went off to use a couple of conventional nets on other sets.

Returning five hours later, when it was quite dark, the net was dropped and the field walked. On our return we found the net had dropped perfectly into the set position, but the result was just two half-grown rabbits enmeshed. Having spent close to fifty years working nets in the traditional manner, I finally solved the

Pre-set drop net in lofted position; note short slide bar supported by release pin (Tony Butler).

Inserting the release pin in the hole below the lofted slide bar with the releasing cord attached to the pin. The head and footlines are attached to the small bobbin fitted to the slide bar (Tony Butler).

Dropping the net from a distance (Tony Butler).

Drop net in its killing position (Tony Butler).

problem of the pre-set nets and the blank sets. It was a purely elementary one.

Setting a couple of old nets lofted on wooden poles, these I suggest we name 'mock nets', we left them, returning each evening until our quarry had completely lost their fear of the unfamiliar object looming overhead and were swarming once again over the set. Replacing the mock nets with the genuine article, on a night when the elements favoured us, we enjoyed a most successful night's use of the pre-set drop net.

I do not think this type of net is widely used, at least, not in Wales, but one may enjoy some success when dropping it prior to darkness falling. My observations are that one requires woodlands to favour this work, and that useful catches may be obtained from an evening drop providing the stretch of wood being worked does not have a similar wood adjacent. In the event of such a piece of cover being in close proximity, rabbits faced with the drop net will turn and seek sanctuary in it.

TIED IN KILL

A number of youngsters may have difficulty in handling the standard type of net, with its free-running netting along the lines, known as 'running-kill' and may opt for nets with meshing tied into the head and foot lines, every eight yards or so. When discussing nets, we in this area refer to the above mentioned type as 'one with tied-in kill'.

Many years ago I did tie the kill in on one of my nets and like others I found that at the tied-in points the mesh bunched up, especially when working an end set. At each point where the tie is made the kill tends to gather in tight balls as the wind blows it along the lines. These knot-like balls, often gather in large sizes and become an embarrassment, especially when wet and may cause the net to become totally inoperable in the event of a twig gathering in the knot. I experienced this very problem, which resulted in the net being snagged up and unable to run off the anchor pin on the following drop. My advice to anyone using tied-in kill who encounters the above-mentioned problem is to free as many of these knots as possible while feeding the net back on to the anchor pin. I must admit I obtained no great advantage from using tied-in kill because each set net is, in effect, tied-in anyway by the restriction imposed on its free-running from every set peg.

Another problem encountered when using tied-in kill is that one finds that the lines will stretch with work. Combined with the odd break that requires repairing, this often results in the head or foot lines becoming shorter in length; consequently the kill gets taut at an angle and the rabbits will bounce off these points. Should one favour tied-in kill, the problem must be addressed by re-adjusting any points of the net necessary prior to a run out. Every man to his own; it may be the net with tied-in kill will be preferred by some, over that of free-running kill.

CARE OF LONG NETS

Considerable time and patience goes into the making of long nets and when September comes round it is these, above all other articles of equipment, that can be relied upon to earn money for the netter's family. When bills were due to be paid one could invariably rely on the nets to settle them. Therefore to enjoy long working lives, regular checking is essential. The odd break should be repaired, otherwise it will soon develop into a larger one when struck by a concentration of rabbits.

An important point to remember about hemp long nets is to make sure they are thoroughly dry before hanging in a cupboard. Leaving hemp nets wet, or even damp, for any length of time is foolish, as they will be ruined by the conclusion of the season. It is also important that one should never dry any net in front of direct heat such as an open fire, or over a radiator. The only safe way to dry a net is to allow the breeze to blow through it, and to enable this to happen the net needs lofting into the air. One may make use of the two clothes-line posts, by fitting a four-foot T-bar across the top of each post and screwing into each T-bar four one-inch diameter self screw-in hooks. The running of the net from hook to hook is then a simple exercise. The breeze will accomplish the rest.

Assuming the long netter works his nets several nights a week, as I often do and a large catch is the result, the odd mesh or two will invariably break. Check the nets for these breaks while airing on the drying hooks. See to it that a net-making needle fully loaded with hemp is on hand so that when a broken mesh is encountered, stretch what remains of it and make it up to its original diamond shape.

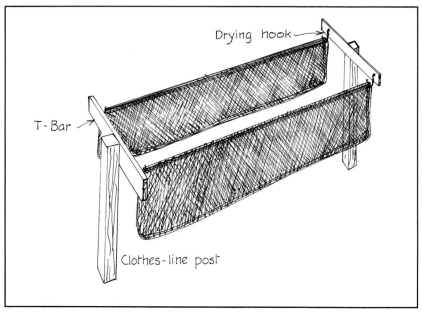

Wet long nets should be lofted clear of the ground to dry. Broken mesh can also be repaired while the net is in this position.

I have my doubts as to whether a professional man would allow his nets to deteriorate through lack of attention. Should he, however, neglect to repair broken meshing, it would cost dearly in loss of rabbits. Even the fact that one does not know how to repair a broken mesh is no excuse. Learn!

Occasionally during the course of a night's work a line will break; more often than not it will be the foot line. An inspection of the break quite often reveals it to be jagged or uneven, indicative of having been bitten by rabbits. If on the other hand the break is a clean one, a rogue poacher could well be the culprit. These men usually cut the head and foot lines, often at the anchor pins. Lines that have been cut at the pins will cause the net to slide down the pegs. This will result in a near blank, because most of the rabbits driven off the field will run over the drooping net. The idea in the mind of the rogue poacher of course, is to hold his opponent up in order that he may work the rest of the sets. I was well briefed by Thomas Moor as to the methods used by these people and was also taught how to handle them.

Having been broken, whether by four-footed, or two-legged creatures, the lines should never be rejoined by means of a knot, for problems will be encountered when running out the net. Instead of a smooth distribution from the anchor pin, the knots will cause the kill to bunch into a ball. More seriously, the net on the pin may tangle on a knotted line and that would render the net useless for the rest of the night.

Repairing a damaged line is a simple matter. Placing both broken ends together, and stitching with a single strand of twelve patent hemp, or two stands of cotton, will allow the kill to run free along the line, as before the breakage.

THE ANCHOR PINS

At either end of the net a steel pin should be attached; these are referred to as 'anchor pins'. Both should measure about nine inches long and be made from quarter-inch stainless steel. One end of each pin should be pointed for the purpose of insertion into the ground. A two-inch diameter ring welded-on previously at the other end, completes each instrument. The purpose of the ring is to allow the net lines to run free. The long net lines should never be tied at the anchor rings – this mistake is often made by the novice. Should the lines be tied at the anchor rings one will find that when run out and pegged down the net will finish up uneven when anchored to the ground. In consequence the set net will lose its tension and sag when struck by rabbits in numbers.

Recently my attention was drawn to a long netting photograph, and what I saw was almost unbelievable. The picture portrayed a man crouching near the anchor pin of a set long net, casting off a dog. On closer inspection, the picture revealed that the head and foot lines of the set net were attached to the ring of the anchor pin in a most unusual manner. The lines were knotted together six inches or so short of the anchor pin ring, a single line then ran to the ring and was tied to it. In my opinion, knots have no place in a long net line. Where breaks have occurred, rejoining by neat stitching is the best remedy. I learned to my cost some time before the Second

27

Anchor pin set in the ground. The head and foot lines run freely through the ring of the pin being joined by stitching. (Tony Butler).

How not to attach the head and foot lines. Note the series of knots and worst of all the knot at the anchor pin ring (David Bishop).

The correct way for the head and foot lines to be attached to the ring of the pin (Tony Butler).

World War that knotted lines can, and do, snag up the net. When being loaded on to the anchor pin the line at the knot gets tangled through a number of meshes and the runner will find the net will not run freely off the pin.

The standard anchor pin can, and does, cause problems for the novice. The problem is referred to as 'going over the back'. This happens prior to running the net out and while it is loaded on to one of the pins. Being two inches in diameter, the pin ring is less than the net mesh in size, so often, while being removed from the equipment used to convey it, the first hank or two may slip over the back.

To say the least, unravelling the net in the dark does not make for the best of humour. Many years ago, a young fellow I took

The net over the back of the anchor pin ring (Tony Butler).

On the left the standard anchor pin ring and on the right the modified and larger ring to stop the net going over the back (Tony Butler).

out on a number of occasions, was beset with this problem of getting the mesh over the back of the ring, but the problem was solved when I supplied him with a special set of pins given to me by Thomas Moor on my initiation into the game. This modified set of pins comprised a ten-inch shaft with a four and three quarter inch diameter ring. The anchor pin ring now being larger than the mesh solved the problem and no longer could the mesh slip over the back. The novice may find this type of pin a valuable addition to his equipment.

LONG NET PEGS

In many years of taking rabbits by making use of long nets, I found two varieties of wood favoured by men of the Wrexham area for making pegs. Occasionally an ash peg was put to use, but most long netters worthy of note favoured a peg cut from a hazel thicket. The diameter of the peg at the end which is to be pointed should be that of a man's index finger. The length should be cut to a measurement that is comfortable for the carrier. Obviously a tall man with long arms is more able to carry a longer peg under his coat in comfort, than a man on the short side. I will give the same advice that I received when first introduced to long netting. The peg should be the length of the user's arm extending from the arm pit to the tips of the fingers when standing to attention. The man standing five feet eight inches tall will normally carry a peg twenty-five inches long, one of greater length is rarely required. I have occasionally used a peg of thirty inches. Of course, when using such a peg I was sinking it into the ground to a depth of ten to twelve inches in order to secure the nets in extremely soft ground. The length of pegs just described are by no means the only ones familiar to me.

I once acquired a forty-yard hemp net of only ten full meshes in depth. In order to create adequate kill, I set the net up on twenty-one inch pegs. This shallow net when set upon these pegs did kill rabbits, but in order to achieve this, the head line was set about fifteen inches from the ground. This setting height proved inadequate when the net was struck by an abundance of rabbits, especially when three or more were tied up between two pegs spaced at five yard intervals. On these occasions I found

31

the net head line pulled flat to the ground by the weight of thrashing rabbits. The result was that the rabbits following simply leaped over these low flattened points into the safety of the cover beyond. I have on occasion read articles by those who should know better, advocating the employment of these short pegs and the spacing of them as far apart as one every eight or ten yards. This policy is sure to lead to the problems I have mentioned. I would not be surprised if those using the short twenty-one inch peg have their head line as taut as a strung bow in order to off-set the above mentioned problems.

At the opposite end of the scale a far worse situation is encountered in the peg of excessive length and thickness. Occasionally during the past few years I have observed 'experts' demonstrating the art of long netting using pegs, or to be more accurate, stakes resembling cricket wickets, three feet or more in length, with a diameter one could only guess at. The manner in which these stakes were conveyed gave rise to the speculation as to whether they were out for a round or two of golf, because the long netter was being instructed to use just that, a golf bag to carry the pegs! How on earth does one expect to move silently along a woodside equipped with a bag on one shoulder containing twenty rattling stakes and hope to set up the nets on these three-foot monstrosities, before the rabbits, with their extremely acute, sensitive hearing, detect the clumsily equipped pair? Add the next complication, of the over-long pegs taking up most of the kill in the nets and we realise such advice must be taken with a pinch of salt.

PEG QUIVERS

From time to time one reads articles concerning the use of long nets, but none has ever described in detail how the pegs are carried. The occasional writer makes a point of mentioning that it requires three men to work the net, one to run the net out, another to peg the net down and the third to carry the bundle of pegs. However, over many years of long netting after my old friend and teacher had passed on, I often worked solo and when working thus, used to run out and peg down three fifty-yard nets as I went along.

It was possible to work the nets solo because we Wrexham

netters employ an article of equipment resembling an archer's quiver. One of these peg containers is easily made from the leg of an old pair of jeans. Having been made it should be stitched on the inside of the long netter's coat along the line of the button holes. The length of coat chosen to accommodate the quiver should reach down the leg to finger tip length, hence the reason for cutting a peg this length. A peg that is too long for the coat to accommodate will cause problems for the netter which could result in a serious accident.

A peg quiver fitted inside the coat (Tony Butler).

I was involved in just such an accident many years ago, when, failing to implement the advice of my old master, I was lucky not to pay too dearly for ignoring the importance of taking particular care. The pegs I was equipped with, reached no higher than the arm pit when placed in the quiver. An old acquaintance, Bill Morgan, and I were setting a harrowed field that had recently been sown, therefore as one may imagine it was very soft. In order to achieve a secure hold for the nets I made use of thirty-inch pegs, as I needed to drive them to a depth of twelve inches in order to feel confident of the net remaining standing when the rabbits struck. I should have constructed a coat and quiver to contain these longer pegs but I had given it a momentary thought and then rejected it.

Consequently, being harnessed with these long pegs in a comparativley short quiver, I was in more danger than I realised. Setting up the first net in the usual smooth manner and having proceeded half way with the second, I received a nasty shock. Having just removed a peg from the quiver and bent down to peg in the net, one of the over-long pegs left point-upwards in its container was driven up one of my nostrils and pierced a blood vessel. Withdrawing the peg I held my head back in the vain hope of checking the flow of blood, but all this achieved was near asphyxia as the blood ran down my throat. At this point I feared the worst, thinking an artery had been severed. But luck was with me – in a while the flow ceased and we were able to continue with our night's work, but not before I had cycled home and re-equipped myself with my twenty-five inch pegs that were tailored for the coat.

In more than fifty years of long netting I have never received any other injury or heard of any other Wrexham netter being injured in an accident such as mine. As long as the coat and peg are measured for the man he should be safe from mishap. One may of course, place the pegs in their receptacle point downwards, but the pegs would soon puncture it full of holes, resulting in a loss of half their number. My advice to the novice netter is, be sure you are correctly equipped. Should this aspect be neglected, one may not be as fortunate as I was and the loss of an eye is a high price to pay for neglecting care and attention to detail.

THE POACHER'S POCKET

The netter is going to require a means to carry his two long nets in comfort. Two men working as a team will equip themselves with identical pieces of carrying equipment.

The following method was and is used still by the professional netters in the Wrexham area. Our two fifty-yard nets are carried in a large pocket which covers the whole width of the coat. The depth should be about sixteen inches and thin canvas is ideal material for the purpose. The pocket starts near the peg quiver and is sewn to the bottom of the coat, the stitching being completed along the bottom and up the side. The use of hemp thread would be most appropriate for the purpose of stitching, as cotton may not be reliable.

Net carrying pockets and peg quiver (Tony Butler).

On completion, the wearer should be able to carry nets and pegs in comfort, one net in either side of the coat. The person equipped in the manner described will have no difficulty in working solo should the need ever arise. Incidentally, the pocket is presumed to be an innovation of the old-time poacher, hence the term 'poacher's pocket'.

—3—

Setting the Long Net

S OME YEARS AGO a young Shropshire man, hearing of
my expertise with the long nets, paid me a visit
accompanied by a friend. I could not very well turn them
away when they said they had been informed of my willingness
to demonstrate the running-out and pegging-down of the long
nets. They had not been misinformed, for I agreed to help
them. Placing my equipment alongside theirs in the vehicle they
were using, I directed them to a nearby field. On arrival I asked
for a demonstration of their expertise. The eager youngsters
were only too pleased to oblige and each strapped a belt from
which hung an archer type quiver round his waist. The peg
receptacle contained several hazel pegs similar in length and
width to the proverbial cricket wickets. They explained that it
was at a game fair that they had learned to equip themselves in
this fashion. They also learned from the same instructor, they
said, how to run out and peg down the long nets.

As we walked along prior to setting up the nets, I pointed out
to them that the racket the pegs were making, banging against
their legs, would soon clear a field of feeding rabbits before half
of the first net was down. These lads at least carried their nets in
a reasonable manner, for each carried a valise on his back,
containing a net apiece. It appeared the runner would take his

partner's net from his valise and run it out, then the pegger removed the runner's net, repeating the process. I pointed out the slowness and tediousness of this method when working solo. It also created more movement than was advisable when setting flat fields, due to the removal of the pack every time a net was required, not to mention the noise created by this extra movement. Sound and movement must be kept to a minimum, I stressed, when working the nets.

The manner in which their nets were run out caused me most amusement. After placing an anchor pin into the ground, the runner ran out the entire length of the net prior to the pegger inserting even a single peg. Inquiring of the runner how he knew when his partner was ready to peg down, his reply was that, having completed the run-out and placed the second pin, the head line was raised as a signal to his partner, who then carried out his part of the process. Upon completion, another net would be removed from the bag and the operation repeated. Here again, I pointed out that he would be unable to work in this fashion in the event of the woodside being dotted with patches of nettles and thistles, not to mention fallen trees. Under these conditions the runner would find the task of running-out the entire net an impossible one. He agreed with my observation, but admitted ignorance as to any alternative method.

I further pointed out that working in their present manner it was easy for the pegger to get a twist in the net and peg down the head line. My companion agreed, saying he had had problems from pegging down the head line. Finally I pointed out the folly of running out the whole net, for it will be laid down over whatever debris lies on the ground, and the nets could become so full of rubbish as to be inoperable for the rest of the night. Prior to picking-up they again foolishly removed every peg from the net whereupon I advised picking up from peg to peg. Realising that carrying out the advice given would keep the problem of dirty nets to a minimum, and having seen my equipment, and also a demonstration of how to drop and pick up the nets, as a team and solo, they did not hesitate to adopt the following methods.

RUNNING-OUT AND PEGGING-DOWN

The person leading the way to set up the nets is called 'the runner'. He will remove one of his two, fifty-yard nets from his poacher's pocket, remove the elastic band that holds the anchor pins together and insert the pin that does not contain the net into the ground. Retreating from the pegger, our runner will make his way along the woodside, feeding the net off the other anchor pin a hank at a time. The runner should maintain a two-peg distance in front of the pegger, approximately ten yards, ascertaining that the lines are taut at all times.

The pegger follows, inserting a peg into the ground every five yards, in order to set the nets firmly in an upright position. This exercise he will find easy to perform as long as he works with the wood behind him. Taking a peg from the quiver he will bend over the net, half-hitch the foot line around the pointed end of the peg and insert the peg into the ground to a depth of about four inches if the ground is firm. Then, taking hold of the top line, which is known as the head line, he will firmly attach it to the top of the peg by means of a double hitch.

Both men will continue with their respective duties until the whole net is run-out and pegged-down. The runner will then insert the anchor pin the net was fed off into the ground. The team will then repeat the procedure. A team of two will usually work four, fifty-yard nets, each man carrying two nets and twenty pegs, ten pegs to each fifty yard net.

For a number of years I have with difficulty kept tongue in cheek when listening to people holding forth on theories pertaining to the long netter's art. Just a few months ago one of these armchair experts made the following statement, 'Few men have the expertise to enable them to run out and peg down a net in a smooth efficient manner, under a cloak of inky blackness.' The reason these novices are unable to work the nets on a black night is due to the fact that they run out and peg down in a like manner to the young pair already mentioned.

A season's practical experience under the tuition of someone as skilled as my old teacher, and any novice would indeed be capable of handling the nets on the blackest night. Furthermore, failing to achieve a standard of excellence in this phase of the art excludes one's chances of ever becoming a

A net loaded onto an anchor pin. Note the rubber band holding the two pins together (Tony Butler).

Inserting the unloaded anchor pin into the ground prior to running the net off the other pin (Tony Butler).

Pegging down the foot line (Tony Butler).

Hitching on the head line. One hitch with the left hand followed by another with the right (Tony Butler).

Head line double hitched onto the peg (David Bishop).

The runner and pegger work as a team, note how the runner keeps the lines tight (Tony Butler).

A set long net, note the billowing of the slack netting known as kill (Tony Butler).

master. One discovers, by venturing out at regular intervals with the nets, that on nights of moderate darkness, because the terrain is favourable, certain sets will yield an abundance of captured rabbits, yet at another set not six hundred yards distant, the yield could be nil. The reason for this is that the last set requires a completely black night in order to produce a successful setting.

One also needs to bear in mind that visiting a set on three nights or so in the same week when the elements are unfavourable, will not only result in a very small capture or the drawing of a blank, which is bad enough, but the major damage done is what is described as 'tricking the set'. Having been tricked, it is advisable to rest the set for three weeks in order that the now educated rabbits have time to forget. Thereafter one should choose a night when the elements favour the netting of the set in question.

In order to attain proficiency in working the nets on a black night two men need to practise an hour or so a day until they become a close, well-rehearsed team. They will then be able to handle nets, no matter how adverse the conditions.

RUNNING-OUT SOLO

Running-out and pegging-down solo is not too difficult provided my instructions are followed, and the technique required is practised before a run out. The method I favour is the one adopted by all the old timers worthy of note in Wrexham. That is, run out with one hand, and peg down with the other. I am unable to drop a net in this manner these days, due to the fact that father time has caused my fingers to lose a great deal of the dexterity they once possessed, but my son and a close friend

43

Charlie Howells, probably two of the best long netters in Wrexham today, still work solo using the following method.

The netter stands with his back to the wood and plants an anchor pin into the ground while the other anchor with the net loaded on is held in the other hand. A yard of the net is then released, this done, a little tension is applied to the head and foot lines by the hand holding the net. All the netter needs to then do is, set the net up on the peg in the normal way, the only difference being that the hitching of the net to the peg will be accomplished with one hand only.

Of course should the ground be hard both hands will be required to insert the peg. When this has to be resorted to, the tip of the anchor pin containing the net will be inserted into the ground at five yard intervals, while the net is set up on a peg. Tension on the head line will be maintained by holding it between clenched teeth, thus leaving one free to peg down with both hands. The set will need to be clean of course in order to employ this method.

PICKING UP THE LONG NETS

The picking up of the nets is very important in the smooth and efficient running out and pegging down of the nets, and I will explain in detail the correct method of picking up. I will first give the method for a team, and second the sequences used when working solo. But my first piece of advice before we tackle our subject is to be sure to remove every button from your coat as failure to do so will result in great frustration as the mesh continuously snags up on them while working the set. Should one wish to close the coat the stitching of draw cords is the best solution.

Picking Up As A Team

When picking up the set nets in pairs, the initial move will be made by the man actually picking up, who will lift an anchor pin from the ground. The next step will be taken by his partner, who will remove the first set peg from the net, place it in its quiver and repeat the operation on the second and third pegs. Having done this he will pause, and place a hand on the head rope in order to feel the tension being applied by his partner picking up. He may also gauge his colleague's progress from reactions transmitted along the head line. One must understand that on a black night both men will be working blind, and therefore their only means of communication will be the net lines.

To resume, the man with the anchor pin in hand will pull toward himself, in order to apply moderate tension to both head and foot lines. This tension is equally as important to successful picking up as running out. Tension applied, the shaft of the pin is placed under the taut lines and a hank of net is slid onto it, the thumb of the hand holding the pin is placed on top of the lines holding the first hank. Reaching out once again with his free left hand he will again take hold, and draw a hank of netting on the pin as he walks forward. As the picker continues this process his partner will not only remove the pegs but raise the foot up to the head line, while taking care to drop the kill of the net between the lines, then it is just a matter of repetition until the net is retrieved.

My advice when picking up in pairs is, never remove every peg from the set net prior to picking up. The problems caused are legion. For instance, should one be working sets that are dirty, ie twigs and brambles strewn about, and lays the entire net on that mess, how on earth can the pick up man deal with the problem without being able to inform his partner? The fact of the matter is, he can't. Especially if said partner races ahead removing pegs from other nets. Yet I have seen this procedure advocated on numerous occasions.

The correct approach to the problem is by working as a close knit, well rehearsed unit, then if the pick up man detects the odd twig in the mesh, the simple signal of three short tugs on the head line will bring his partner poste haste to help sort out the problem. This accomplished, both will continue with their respective duties. One will agree, I am sure, that what I have just described is a far superior system to removing every set peg prior to picking up.

Picking up the long net by feeding back onto an anchor pin a hank at a time (Tony Butler).

Picking the net up from peg to peg (Tony Butler).

Returning a peg to its quiver while picking up the net (Tony Butler).

Completing the process of picking up the long net (Tony Butler).

Picking Up Solo

Having become proficient at working the nets as part of a team, one may occasionally wish to run solo. The picking up of the set nets will prove to be a simple task.

One begins as when working as part of a team by picking up an anchor pin. Then applying a little pressure to the lines by pulling. Then with the free hand remove the first peg from the net and continue along as one normally would when working as a team, placing each peg on removal into its quiver. Peg to peg, one will find this method of picking up simple to achieve. The common practice among the professionals in my day was to retrieve one's own nets in the above described manner unless, of course, the sets were known to be dirty.

ENCOUNTER WITH A WOODSMAN

An incident worth mentioning happened a few nights before a Christmas Eve some years ago. My son Arthur and I were setting a long fir wood know to us as 'The Mill Sets'. Walking out to beat the field after setting up the nets, I saw the wax and wane of the glow from a lighted cigarette as the smoker moved in our direction, not a hundred yards distant. Alerting Arthur by sounding the double click signal with the tongue, to warn of possible trouble, I informed him of my observation. His decision was to wait on the end of the nets and intercept the smoker. The net covered a gateway into the wood leading to Mr Jones, the gamekeeper's, release pens.

Crouching silently near the gate, we waited until the intruder was almost upon us, then rising like shadows out of the ground, prepared for combat if the stranger felt so inclined, challenged him. To say the least, his first reaction was startled surprise, for his strangled cry took even me aback. Arthur decided a straight forward approach was the correct policy, saying 'Careful where you place your feet pal, as I have a net covering this gateway.' The reply came in the form of a question. 'Have you received permission from Mr Jones the keeper to take rabbits from this estate?' My answer was 'I can do better than that, I carry a written request from the administrators to reduce the rabbit population, of course with the head keepers approval.'

The stranger gave me the impression that if he was not exactly a night hawk, he was at least a kindred spirit, explaining that he worked for the estate as a woodsman and general handyman. The reason for his presence in the covert at this late hour, he imparted, was to collect half a dozen trees. They were just inside the gate covered by our first net. Stepping over it he silently entered the wood and in a very short time returned with half a dozen Christmas trees, saying 'I have a sale for these.' Then, laying them down, said, 'I have often hoped to observe real long netters at work.' 'Welcome,' said I, 'sit by me' and sent Arthur out to clear the field while I waited with young Phil, as the woodsman's name turned out to be, on the nets. In a short time I could feel the rabbits striking the nets, one or two emitting screams of fear on becoming enmeshed. The manner of dispatchment of the first rabbit seemed to fascinate him. He informed me that a shot rabbit, if not dead, was put out of its pain with a 'rabbit punch'.

Running out and pegging down a net with a white head line and a green foot line (David Bishop).

Later he informed me that he had tried long netting on a couple of occasions but was plagued by the mesh going over the back. After I explained the reason for this problem and how to solve it, by having the anchor pin ring larger than the mesh, he said 'There is something else; I was getting the nets hopelessly tangled.' I told him these problems affected most learners and the answer to prevent the lines from becoming so twisted as to be inoperable for most of the night, was to keep the head and foot lines separate and taut at all times. That is the runner's responsibility, but as this problem will often present itself for learners, I said the only sure way to avoid any confusion in the mind of the pegger, when presented with a slack section of line laid along the ground, is to have a white head line and a green foot line. A net rigged in this fashion leaves the novice in no doubt as to which is the head line.

The suggestion I have made as to the colour of the head line will of course be of little value on a black night. The work will invariably be performed by feel alone upon such a night, but the white head line will be a great help when working in moderate darkness and the young man working solo will find its value inestimable until such time as he becomes an experienced practitioner.

Another problem commonly met by the novice, I told young Phil as I poured him a cup of hot coffee from my flask, is that of sections of the net being flattened by striking rabbits. This is the result of nets being set up on pegs poorly secured into the ground and one usually encounters this problem following a hot dry summer.

When pegging down the nets, it is important to lay the pegs slightly back towards the woods and away from the striking rabbits in order to create a natural billowing of the kill in the bottom of the net. Laying the pegs at the angle described will also be advantageous to the learner and experienced long netter alike, when they come to pick up the nets, for they will discover the advantage of the foot line being set slightly forward of the head line, thus enabling one to raise the foot line to the head line as one picks up the nets, allowing the kill to automatically drop between the lines.

Now when the ground is hard, one has no alternative but to lay the pegs at the opposite angle, ie away from the wood. One

When the ground is hard one has to lay the pegs away from the wood and towards the striking rabbits (David Bishop).

Twisted lines caused by pegging down the head line where the foot line should be (David Bishop).

finds that laying the pegs at this opposite angle on bone-hard ground practically eliminates the problem of sections of the net being flattened by striking rabbits. But, pegging down at this angle does make for slower picking-up because the head line, now being in advance of the foot line, tends to cause the kill between the lines to fall the wrong side of the foot line, whereas it should always fall between the two lines, otherwise a real mess may result on the following set.

When in use, over-deep nets cause their owners a number of problems. Chief among these is the entangling of the feet in the kill as the wind blows against them. One may insist that these men are extremely clumsy, but the fact is they exist. The only alternative for these unfortunates is to face the wood when pegging down and have the wind striking their backs and blowing the web away from their feet. This method has its drawbacks, however, being slower than that used by most professionals. The pegger has to place the head line over the back of his head, and there are two reasons for this – firstly, for the purpose of separating the head and foot lines, and secondly

An alternative method of pegging down the long net (Tony Butler).

to allow the pegger easy access to the foot line. I have used this method and found it most uncomfortable, particularly in wet weather, also the placing of head line over the head can become extremely tiresome, because in the event of one wearing a cap, as I do, it is frequently whipped off by the taut head line. This method, in my opinion, should only be used as a last resort.

END SETTING

Let us now turn our attention to setting the wind that blows directly down the side of the wood. It should be directly in the long netters' faces as they walk down the woodside.

The wind blowing at this angle is called end-setting. My preference invariably has been to work long stretches of woodland on a wind that blows between the end and plump sets, accepting the plump wind as due south. The end set will be either east or west. My preference is a south-east, or south-west wind as this semi-end setting will make allowance for any twists or turns the wood may take. When working an end set the pegger will find that the wind will blow the kill down the lines, bunching it at one end, therefore it is important that he is constantly pulling and rearranging the amount of kill between each peg. Another point to remember is, having finished the set, that he should be sure to pick up the nets with the wind in his face. When picking up thus, the netter will find that the kill is more evenly distributed along the lines. Should he attempt to pick up with the wind at his back, the wind will blow the kill away from him and unnecessary work will have been created on the following set, feeding the kill back along the lines while pegging down.

TAILING AND LINKING

Occasionally, magazine articles have caught my eye written by people professing expert knowledge on the long netting art, but after reading them I have come to the conclusion that the real art was still a mystery to the writers. A season's long netting with Thomas Moor or Jack Ginger, to mention but two, and they would have understood the real art of long netting. The reason Thomas and Jack were so highly regarded was because of their ability to vary their style of net setting to suit the elements prevailing and the terrain being worked. Many of today's pseudo experts conclude erroneously that all a long netter requires is the wind blowing in the correct direction, allowing the setting up of nets on a particular set he has in mind, and the rabbits will gallop in like lambs to the slaughter. Few are aware that the rabbits that bounce off their shop-bought nets, that are sadly lacking in kill, and run the whole length to enter the cover beyond, can be captured quite easily. The answer is the 'tailed' net.

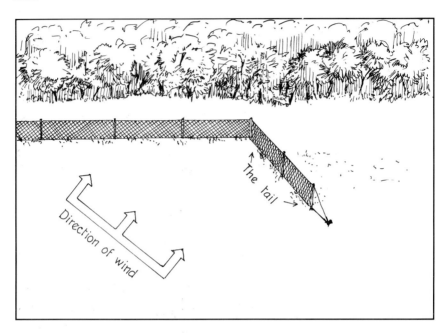

Tailing the first fifteen or twenty yards of the first set net mid-way along a section of woodland.

My first instruction in the long netter's art proved invaluable in after-years, for it was on this occasion I learned 'linking' and 'tailing', but most importantly I was made aware of the reasons for using these methods. Leading the way through a hunting gate, Thomas whispered in my ear 'Give me one of your nets, Harold.' Having complied with this request, I followed. After moving along the field for perhaps a hundred yards he halted. Removing the elastic band that held the anchor pins together, he placed it in the palm of my hand for safekeeping; it would be needed when the net was retrieved later. I expected my companion to insert the first pin into the ground close to the woodside. Instead he walked directly out into the field for a distance of about fifteen yards, stopping below the brow of the hill that ran the whole length of the field, keeping us blind from the feeding rabbits.

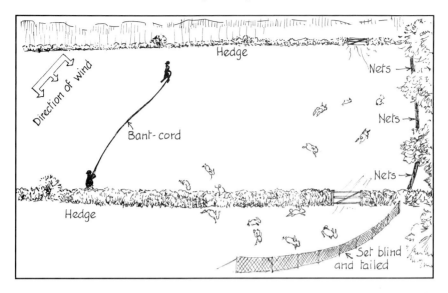

One net tailed blind behind a hedge and a further three nets run out in the traditional manner on an adjoining field and along the woodside.

At this point he inserted the pin into the ground then ran the net directly back towards the woodland. Practically retracing his footsteps, I followed, pegging the net down. Arriving back close to the woodside he ran the rest of the net out in the regular fashion. Taking my second net out I handed it to Thomas. We were standing behind the last peg of the first set net and he inserted the anchor pin of the second net into the ground in front of the first set net. The head line of this second net was double hitched to the top of the last peg of the first set net, the foot line of this linking point was left free as we continued to run out and pegged-down in the traditional manner, by using a half hitch round the pointed end of the peg with the foot line, followed by a double hitch round the top of the peg with the head line.

The above-mentioned method of linking and pegging the long nets was repeated by Thomas with every net run out. Of course it is only the first end that is tailed. All four nets being set he said 'Harold, that is how a professional long netter tails and links his nets.' As we proceeded to drive the rabbits home he explained the reason for tailing and linking the long nets. His reason for walking the first hundred yards of the set before

55

Linking the nets. Note the large anchor pin and that the head line only of the second net is linked onto the last peg of the first set net (Tony Butler).

setting the long net was because he had killed heavily on it on several occasions earlier in the season, but to help cover the hundred-yard gap, especially when end-setting, it was wise to tail the first set net. By doing so, any rabbit that had to travel out into the wind from below the first set net, would in his opinion often travel into the prevailing wind, that is why the tailing of the first net is vital when end-setting.

There were also a number of important reasons why the long nets were linked. The first and more obvious of these was that less pegs were needed, but most importantly, linking the nets reduces the risk of a rogue poacher following on behind and cutting the lines, or even trying to steal your first set net while you may be pegging down the fourth. Any vibrations travelling along the lines of the first net will be transmitted along the whole four nets. The experienced netter knows that vibrations signify rabbits in the nets, or someone helping themselves to a valuable net.

Another reason for linking the nets is that the rabbits can find no gap to push through. On this particular night we enmeshed thirty-three on the first set and eleven were killed in the tail. On the second set eighteen were caught, five of these were in the tail of the first net. Over many years of netting, I found the tailing of the first net when end-setting, often had considerable bearing on the outcome of the number of rabbits taken in a night's work.

A ROGUE POACHER

Jack Ginger was a long netter *par excellence* and from time to time would run out for a night's long netting with another first-class exponent of the art, Harry Crowther. Jack had a great deal of respect for Harry's outstanding abilities with the long nets and in his opinion Harry was one of the cleverest netters he had ever run with, but as with most men, Harry was found wanting in one respect. He was an extremely jealous person, and Jack told me of two occasions when Harry demonstrated his failing.

The first instance was when they cycled out to an estate some six miles from Wrexham, and situated near the banks of the River Dee. Lifting the cycles over a gate, both moved along a hedge seeking safe concealment for their transport. What they came across was not to Harry's liking. Tucked in against the hedge were two more cycles. Both machines he recognised as belonging to Wrexham netters. Jack said he had great difficulty in preventing his companion from throwing the opposition's transport into the river just two hundred yards away. Harry took a lot of persuading, but eventually agreed to leave things as they were. Both men moved on a couple of miles to another estate and enjoyed a successful night. After this experience Jack confided that he never concealed his transport anywhere where Harry might stumble upon it.

Jack now knew that in the event of his being out with other company Harry, arriving second on the set, could, in his rage, resort to a number of well-tried tricks. There was in fact, a later occasion, when Harry played a rascally trick on Jack Ginger and Dewi. Harry was known to the fraternity as a rogue poacher. He was, of course, not on his own. Competing teams of netters would use their guile in an effort to out-smart the men first on the sets.

One dark, windy night, Jack and Big Dewi were setting on a benevolent north-north westerly wind. The set was at the bottom of a very long woodland. On the first set, they accounted for thirty-eight rabbits, but were rewarded with blanks on the following two sets. 'Dewi,' said Jack, 'someone has crossed these sets.' 'Not necessarily' said Dewi. 'It may have been a fox. Still we may as well satisfy ourselves and investigate the possibility that someone is deliberately spoiling the sets for us.' Thereupon they made for the last set on the ground. It also happened to be the best set on the estate, being known to the night hawks as the 'stable set'. As they approached they were greeted by the screams of rabbits enmeshed in the long nets. Squatting at the end of the last net, both men waited patiently for what they now knew to be a rogue poacher.

After a short while, a single figure could be seen on the skyline, moving quickly down the line of nets, chinning the rabbits. Jack said it was no surprise to come face to face with Harry Crowther, working solo. It was a nasty surprise for him, being caught red-handed, so to speak. He swore he would never have turned rogue on Jack and Dewi had he known it was they who were setting the estate. He was given the benefit of the doubt, but not before Dewi had taken him by the scruff of the neck and shaken him until his teeth rattled. Whether this had any effect on Harry's future conduct is debatable, and, despite that incident, the three ran out together on many occasions for thirty years or more.

Jack said Harry was such a fine poacher and likeable character he just could not help being drawn to him. I understood Jack perfectly, for in my lifetime I have met a number of people who possessed what I call a 'dark streak'; I realised there was a limit as to how far they could be trusted, but in spite of their defects I just could not help liking them.

—4—

Driving Home the Quarry

HAVING SET UP the nets, the next task is the driving home of the quarry. I advise the uninitiated not to walk out on to the feeding ground, but instead to take a wide arc round the perimeter of the feeding ground in order to place themselves well up-wind of their prey. It must be remembered that on a mild, cloudy night, rabbits will travel a number of fields from the home woods, if there is feeding far out to their liking. Therefore it would be a mistake to range the field in close proximity to the woods, and exclude the fields in the rear. Having arrived well out on the feeding grounds, the two men should range the fields from left to right back towards the set nets. This ranging of the fields is colloquially termed by the Wrexham long netters as 'banting'.

SOUND BANTING

It is advisable to 'sound bant', by slapping one's Wellington boot with a spare peg, or alternatively shake half a box of matches. This will ensure that most of the feeding rabbits will be startled and make for the waiting nets, minus the odd couple. These will squat and remain out on the feeding ground. I must make it clear that employing the sound-banting method excludes the

59

use of the human voice, because of its penetrating quality over considerable distances, therefore the human voice cannot be considered as an effective banting instrument. One needs mild unfamiliar sound, the human scent will do the rest.

On the premise that the sets being worked are no more than a couple of hundred yards apart, the pair banting would be wise to give the field no more that a wide, brisk quartering up wind of the feeding rabbits and silently bant the set. Alternatively, another form of banting, the 'bant cord', may be used to suit this type of ground of which more in a minute.

To stress the point that the human voice is anathema to long netters at work, my son and I were recently plagued by this problem while working a number of sets which had a lane running past in close proximity, and having killed well on a south-facing set close to the lane, were about to wind up operations on this first of three drops when a car containing a number of what sounded like drunk and certainly rowdy, occupants, pulled up in the lane, disgorging its drunken crew. They climbed aboard again in a very short time and moved on. Following their departure and against my better judgement I foolishly dropped the net on the next set instead of returning after a lapse of four hours and yes, reader, you are right, I drew a blank. So my strong advice is to refrain from raising one's voice, or for that matter using it at all when driving home the rabbits.

THE DOUBLE BANT

It was my teacher, Thomas Moor, who demonstrated the importance of the 'double bant', also various forms of this phase of the art. My introduction to it was some time before the Second World War. He and I were working a set known as 'The Boards', an excellent banky, or blind, set it proved to be. It is ideal for the topic under discussion. We were working with a quarter moon on the rise, with a thick patch of cloud passing over intermittently, dulling the silver brightness, and a fresh wind to aid us. We erected our nets along the woodside and with a convenient thick patch of cloud obscuring the moon, got well out to bant.

Returning to the nets, which were full of enmeshed rabbits, I noticed the moon peeping out from the tail end of the cloud, turning relative darkness into a kind of silver twilight. The sight, combined with the silence and solitude, engendered in me feelings that were inexplicable, but years later when reading the Good Book, the incident was made clear when I read of 'The Peace that passeth all understanding' and I thank whatever gods may be for just that one moment.

However, to get back to the matter in hand. A number of rabbits homeward bound and clearly visible on the horizon, stopped and sat up on their haunches, probably half a dozen of the old guard who had become educated. I noted as one or two of their enmeshed comrades gave a scream of fear these wise old soldiers turned about and ran back onto their feeding ground, squatting to wait the passing of the danger that lay between them and the safety of the home covert. As we disposed of the catch and proceeded to extract them from the nets, I informed Thomas of my observations. His reply was 'Those rabbits have probably encountered poorly constructed nets, bounced off and become 'tricked'; we will give them half an hour to calm down.' This we did, passing the time legging the rabbits on to slings.

Transporting rabbits legged onto slings.

The appropriate time had passed before we both ventured out to bant the field once more. The result was a further eight rabbits ending up in the nets. Thus my old master taught me the value of double banting. Dawn was about to break and it had been a profitable night's work yet Thomas dropped the nets for the last time on a set covered with rough grass, patches of thistles and nettles. Twenty-eight were caught up in them, yet my companion insisted on the 'dawn bant', but not before we had tailed both ends of the set nets in an effort to prevent the educated rabbits from running their entire length and on to safety. From this final and second bant a further twelve ended in the nets.

THE BANT CORD

Assuming the woods being set are long, with fields split up at regular intervals by hedgerows, I would advise end-setting and no 'sound bant'. Fields so closely adjacent require the use of the 'bant cord'. It may be made up of lines taken from old long nets stitched together to a length of about two hundred yards. The finished article is wound onto a spindle.

Running out the bant cord (Tony Butler).

Both men first walk to the far end of the field about to be dragged. One holds the spindle while his partner takes hold of the free end. This end must contain a loop through which the runner-out can place his hand, to ensure the line does not pull out of his hand when the drag commences. Having dragged the cord over the ground up to the set nets, the spindle holder rewinds while his partner despatches the enmeshed rabbits.

CHINNING THE RABBITS

The rabbits having become enmeshed in the net, now need dispatching, so I will explain the chinning method used. Having mentioned the word on a number of occasions it is time I defined it, to save further bewilderment for the reader.

It is an easy matter to remove the rabbits from the nets when dead, but taking them out when still alive is not so easy. The live rabbit tends to bunch up into a tight ball, therefore it is wise to dispatch it while still tied up in the kill of the net. This is carried out in the following manner. Take hold of the creature from behind, completely encircling its neck with one hand. Place the palm of the other hand under the rabbit's chin then with a quick movement push the head upward and back. Death will then follow instantly.

Chinning a rabbit.

I have read in a number of books pertaining to poachers and poaching a considerable amount of what amounts to rubbish on the subject of long netting. It is obvious to me and any experienced netter, that these authors possess very little practical knowledge of the long netter's art. Most, when describing the method used to dispatch an enmeshed rabbit, talk of making use of a torch or lantern in order that the poacher may see to dispatch the rabbits by making use of a short cudgel to strike the creature on the head. This sort of nonsense convinces me of their lack of practical experience and whatever they do possess is unskilled to say the least. It would be fatal for a poacher to shine a torch on any pretext, along a woodside. Any gamekeeper worth his salt would have anyone as foolish as this in the Magistrate's Court.

The dispatching of rabbits should be carried out in complete darkness, by feel only. Chinning is the skilled man's method. I once observed a so-called expert pick up a rabbit by its back legs and strike it across the back of the neck. The resultant bruise to the shoulder and back rendered most of it inedible.

—5—

The Long Netter's Dog

S HE WAS BLACK in colour, and of poor conformation, standing twenty inches at the shoulder with poorly muscled hind legs. This lack of muscular development was the obvious reason for her lack of speed. Down the left side of the rib cage one could trace a six-inch scar, acquired while in the ownership of gypsies. Sired by a small black whippet cross, out of a poorly shaped labrador whippet cross, she was not only the best long netting dog I ever possessed, but the best I ever saw. Coming into my ownership at four years of age, she was already a very experienced bitch, having been passed on by gypsies to a long netter of my acquaintance who named her Brandy and broke her in a masterful manner to meet his requirements. Harsh, rather than cruel, was my opinion of his training method. Dogs under his control soon learned that to step out of line brought swift and painful retribution.

It was the owner of Brandy who instructed me in the art of training a dog to drive the rabbits into the long nets. My first priority, he said, was to obtain a dog of consistent temperament. In his opinion an excitable one was ill-equipped for the task. I was also informed that the trainer should never in the initial stages of training, allow his charge to drive into the nets, or ever catch a rabbit at all. It was made clear that the task of the dog was not to tear after the first rabbits raised in the dark. His was a specialist skill, therefore it was of paramount importance that the temptation to chase a single rabbit be resisted and the ranging and quartering of the fields from side to side should be uninterrupted, thereby raising the feeding rabbits and ushering them toward the waiting nets.

In my estimation, any long netting dog worthy of the name will not attack a single victim in the nets. It is also important that the dog does not 'break the field' because the netter may wish to set the adjacent one. A dog possessing the flaw of breaking field is better left at home.

TRAINING

Training a dog to work the nets should be carried out in separate stages. If the subject cannot, or will not, obey the commands 'sit' and 'stay' then it will be useless for its intended purpose, as its duties must be performed in the dark and, upon completion, it must stay put for an hour if need be. The commands 'sit' and 'stay' should be given from between clenched teeth and amount to a soft hissing sound in the dog's ear. The futility of raising one's voice in order to give a command is obvious, for a verbal command would immediately clear the field of rabbits, and possibly the adjacent one also.

My dogs were taught to sit and stay by means of a simple ritual. Placing its meal in front and pressing its haunches down, I gave the accompanying order 'sit'. Having attained and held the position for twenty seconds the dog was allowed to eat, by snapping the fingers with the command 'get on'. Having persuaded the trainee to remain steady to the 'sit', I accompanied the order with a hissing sound in its ear and in a very short time the subject would sit to the hiss alone. Steady now in front of its food, the dog was taken to a nearby field where its 'sit' and 'stay' training was extended. By giving the order and moving back five yards, in the event of the dog following it would be dragged back, given a little rough handling and a harsh word. When the order was obeyed, a biscuit and kindly pat was the reward. The training was continued until the command, once given, was obeyed long after I had disappeared from sight.

Sit And Stay At The Long Nets

When steady to the 'sit' and 'stay' order, the trainee was taken to a local field and sat down at the woodside, while I ran out a fifty-yard net, continuing with the procedure until the dog sat steady throughout the period taken to run out and peg down four more nets, also the retrieving of them. Having arrived at this stage of its education, I gave it its first banting lesson. Being steady by this time to the 'sit' and 'stay' at the anchor pin of the first net run out, I took it to a field known by me to contain no rabbits. Sitting the dog in the manner taught, I ran out a long net along the woodside. This accomplished, I returned and calling the dog by name gave the order to bant, which is simply 'get on'. The trainer will find it expedient to encourage the animal by walking out and quartering the field with it when returning to the nets – quartering is a left-to-right movement across the field, all the way back to the net – thereafter returning the dog to the initial anchor pin, giving the appropriate command prior to picking up the nets.

It is of vital importance that the young dog has a thorough understanding of the command 'no'. The netter will find the word invaluable in checking the trainee whenever tempted to chase off wildly after any rabbit raised. It is also an important restrainer in the event of an attack on enmeshed rabbits. A reliable method of teaching the command 'no' is by making use of 'baits.' The handler is required to sit his charge with a lead attached to its collar, throw a bait in front of it and any attempt to move should be countered by a sharp tug on the lead accompanied with the order 'no'. An intelligent animal will not require many such lessons in view of the fact that at an earlier stage it was taught to sit in front of a meal and not partake until receiving the command 'get on'.

Ignoring The Enmeshed Rabbits

The dog is now steady on the 'sit' and 'stay' at the long net and also has a good understanding of the order 'no' and that 'get on' means his release from the 'sit' and 'stay' position, allowing it to proceed with its task of quartering the field. It is now imperative that the dog be taught to 'honour' the enmeshed

A long netting dog in the correct position at the first anchor pin while the nets are run out and set. Note also how the pegs are laid slightly back towards the wood (David Bishop).

Casting off the dog (David Bishop).

The dog thoroughly bants the field back toward the set nets (David Bishop).

After completing the bant: the dog in the correct position while the nets are picked up (David Bishop).

rabbits, that is refrain from mauling the prey in the nets.

The most successful and quickest results will be achieved by introducing the dog to enmeshed rabbits. It would be preferably in the summer months, in daylight, that this be done. A field of long rough grass will invariably contain a few squatting rabbits. Having driven these into the net one should move in with the dog on lead and when an attempt is made to snap at one of the captives, the handler will utter the command 'no' in a harsh voice, take the dog by the scruff giving a firm shake and repeating the command while dispatching the rabbits. The dog should then be returned to the spot where the first net was run out and remain on the 'drop' until the booty has been removed from the nets, legged on to slings and the nets secured ready for moving on. During all this time the dog must sit steady 'on the drop'.

Banting By Moonlight

Our trainee is now ready to be tested on the night of a full moon. A blind set with a steep bank is ideal for this phase of the training. Having followed the same procedure as during daylight, that is, bant the field with dog on lead and remove any rabbits enmeshed, the dog may then be released to bant the field free of any restriction while the handler returns to the nets. His young charge should be rewarded with a pat and kind word on return.

Proficiency by moonlight having been achieved, the last hurdle looms ahead, namely to bant in darkness, honour the nets and not break field. You should allow the young dog to bant just one set each night during the first season, as too much work too soon is sure to result in a breakdown in steadiness.

SELECTING A DOG

Many lurchers are not suitable for this type of training as a dog is required possessing a very high trainability factor and certain natural instincts. I have known exceptions, like Brandy, and perhaps the most suitable lurcher would be a collie/greyhound cross.

The working sheepdog is a breed I have never employed as a

70

banter to the nets. Nevertheless, with its inherent instinct for making a wide outrun of a field, which we in the long netting fraternity refer to when discussing the banting dog as 'the strike round', also the natural instinct to drive back toward its master, are virtues in themselves and prompt me to suggest the breed is a desirable one, especially in view of its wellknown high trainability factor coupled with its inborn herding instinct. I have found a Labrador crossed springer adequate, the springer's natural instinct for quartering being the deciding factor.

It must be borne in mind that training to bant is a specialised subject and at the conclusion the animal must be one hundred per cent steady – ninety-nine is not good enough.

Brandy

Over the many years of my long netting activities, I worked with only three superb banting dogs and when the opportunity of acquiring Brandy presented itself I was overjoyed. I have already introduced you to this remarkable bitch, but neither I, nor anyone else, would have come into possession of her, had not her unfortunate owner met with an accident which left him with multiple leg breaks and serious pelvic injuries. On receiving information that he intended to sell his dogs, I approached him and Brandy came into my ownership for five pounds. There was more than a suspicion of a tear in the fellow's eye when he handed her over and said 'Be kind to her, Harold.' I felt guilty and turned my head away as I gave my promise.

I expected Brandy to be a little restless for a few days, after purchase, but the problem never occurred. From the very first day, she made herself at home, was spotlessly clean and was a 'good grubber', which means she would eat anything digestible. After a few weeks of getting acquainted we became firm friends and on our fairly regular jaunts locally she always came up with a rabbit for the pot, even without Lady, the springer that used to bush for her. Her captives were killed in a manner unique to her – she took her prey by the head and crushed it with a single bite.

The initial night of banting with Brandy took place in the company of my eldest son and I must confess, this night of long netting became a memorable one. There was more to it than the excellent manner of the banting. It was a night of no moon, but the sky was thick with white cloud which shed sufficient light to enable us to work in comfort. The weather was dry, with a fresh south-easterly breeze. We crossed the border into the county of Shropshire, where the woods we were mindful of setting were known to us as 'the rollers'. Arriving at close to midnight we parked in close proximity to the woods.

The first set was a short blind one requiring only three or four nets. Once on set, a gentle hiss in Brandy's ear and she immediately sat. I ran out the nets and my son followed pegging the net down. The task accomplished, we returned to the first and were pleased to find the little black bitch sitting rock steady in her appointed place. We had decided I was to stay on the nets while my son and Brandy banted the field. Our intention was to verify the fact that the bitch banted back towards the nets. Pulling out into the wind when in receipt of a whiff of the scent of feeding rabbits is a common fault with many a long netting dog.

The experienced practitioner will take a wide sweep getting well out, then bant in toward the waiting net, for he is well aware that the killing will take place there. Holding the head line of the first net, I felt it quiver in my hand. Quietly I walked the net holding the head line, until arriving at the first enmeshed rabbit. Dispatching it, I carried on, and by the time the last net was reached I had eliminated thirteen more. Walking back to meet my son I heard the crunch of bone and thought, what a waste of time, for I knew it was Brandy. Mistakenly I came to the conclusion that the bitch was mutilating the rabbits I had killed. However, after bellying up the catch on removal from the nets, we counted eighteen, whereas I had killed thirteen. Upon inspection we found five bearing Brandy's trademark, crushed heads, and we were well pleased, because it proved she only treated live rabbits in this manner.

I enquired of my son as to the style in which the bitch went about her work. 'Brilliant', was the answer. He had been crouching below the brow of the hill in order to facilitate the sighting of the bitch coming over the skyline, he said 'Dad, she came over the skyline cruising like a yacht before the wind, banting the ground thoroughly.' A very apt description, I thought.

Having legged and hung the catch in the branch of a tree in order to protect them from predators, we moved on and completed three more settings. Allowing the bitch to do all the work while we crouched at the nets waiting for the rabbits to strike, a good deal of leg work was saved that night. The capture of thirty-four rabbits on the final three sets, brought the total take for the night to fifty-two.

The rabbits should be legged onto slings and hung out of the reach of vermin.

Returning to our vehicle, we found a reception waiting. At a hundred yards distant from the van, Brandy suddenly trotted a few yards ahead and halted, ears pricked. She uttered a low growl. Running my hand gently from neck to withers, I felt the hair standing and knew the potential enemy was hiding close by. My son was about to insert the key into the van door when five figures materialised from the surrounding cover – the head keeper, two under-keepers, a farm labourer and a policeman from a nearby village. All appeared to have loaded sticks in their possession.

At the sight of me the head keeper's mouth fell open in surprise and then I realised the whole incident was my fault. I had forgotten to 'phone-in the fact that the registration number of the van was different from the one we gave the estate the year before, as we had changed the vehicle. Naturally we were assumed to be poachers and forces were generated to deal with the situation. When the mix-up was sorted out our parting was amicable. William, the old keeper, sadly long deceased, had many a laugh when that fiasco was discussed.

—6—

The Moon, Wind Direction and Other Tips

BY THE TIME I was well along the road to becoming a fully qualified long netter, I struck up a friendship with a man who bore the pseudonym 'Bob the Ice Cream'. He also was no mean exponent of the netter's art. Although he worked legally, Bob was not averse to a little poaching, given the opportunity and the right set of circumstances. But it is to his credit that when working outside the law, he always worked solo, preferring not to saddle any colleagues with the consequences of being apprehended.

One night we travelled to some very good sets, known as 'The Trotting Mare', some ten miles from Wrexham. As was often the case, our only means of transport was to cycle. Two miles along the road my rear tyre burst. Bob was surprised when I said 'No matter, I'll run beside you to the 'Trotting Mare''. Placing the cycle behind the hedge and handing my coat containing equipment to Bob, I ran the eight miles that remained. After killing thirty-four bunnies and legging them onto slings for my partner to arrange as best he could on the bar, and any other part of the cycle capable of carrying, but retaining my jacket with nets and pegs, I found the return journey a fairly easy exercise. Bob's was a far more difficult proposition. Even with some fair stretches of road, hilly and suitable for fast free-

75

wheeling, I inevitably caught up and was on hand to give a little help when called upon.

THE MOON

Travelling out to the same sets a fortnight later was a different kettle of fish, so to speak. A half moon was just beginning to climb in a broken clouded sky to the south-east. Our work had to be completed before the moon climbed even higher sending its silvery brightness from a south-westerly position. We were of course prepared for this. The experienced long netters of yesteryear were well acquainted with the embarrassments caused by the moon's phases and made it their business to be able to predict accurately the time of the moon's rising and its position in the sky. It was no coincidence that on this night we had travelled out to set the side of the woods facing north-west, or that we were working on a north-westerly breeze. This side of the wood was in dark shadow along its covert side for thirty or forty yards, but we also knew just how long it would take for the mistress of the sky to replace that shadow with brilliant light. Under these conditions speed was of the essence and of paramount importance to the success, or failure, of the night's exercise. We were racing against the inevitable loss of our shadow cover and knew to within a matter of ten minutes when that would be. Yes, knowing the phases of the moon and how to capitalise on the knowledge is important.

Contrary to popular beliefs held by the long netters of yesteryear, who thought the new moon was a crescent moon, it is amazing how many netters still think that the waxing crescent moon is the new moon, when most of us now know that when 'her ladyship' is directly between the earth and the sun, rendering her invisible to the naked eye, it is then she is the new moon and it is during the phase of the new moon that the netter has all the advantage.

I would advise huntsmen of every description to study the moon and its phases, if only for its educational value. It should certainly interest any lover of nature to learn how the harvest moon got its name and why. The same goes for a hunter's moon. If one admits the moon's capability of controlling certain of the Earth's physical functions such as controlling the tides of

76

the seas, then it could well be that as man is, it is said, seventy-five per cent water, that the moon may exert a certain amount of influence on his behaviour.

PREDICTING WIND DIRECTIONS

An important phase of the long netter's development is that of predicting the wind. As a learner of the great game, he must have the means whereby accurate prediction is possible. He must know when the wind will be striking a particular side of a wood. It is of little use two people spending time and energy setting up nets along the woodside if their scent is blown out on to the feeding field. Working thus can result only in blank sets and empty nets. The netter must have the wind blowing from the feeding rabbits in the direction of the set nets and they should be billowing away from the striking rabbits.

To predict accurately the direction of a particular wind, the wise novice team will equip themselves with a compass before venturing forth with the nets and visit the ground they intend to set. Equipped with the compass, notebook and pen, one of them should stand with his back to the wood they intend to set, facing the field the rabbits feed on and, taking a reading from the compass to ascertain the wind required, pencil it down in the note book. For instance, should the needle point in the direction of the feeding field and indicate due south, the netter will require a wind blowing from the south to plump set that particular side of the wood. In my opinion, accurately predicting the direction a particular wind will strike cannot be overstressed.

I have read and listened to men claiming to be experienced long netters and their method for predicting the wind accurately amounted to sheer nonsense. One writer possessed a reasonable method. He learned where north, south, east and west winds struck his house and, from this knowledge, claimed the ability to travel to his setting ground and find the wind as he predicted. But he made no mention of his reaction should the wind change direction while en route, and I have suffered this phenomenon on a number of occasions.

Let us look now at the alternatives to the compass for predicting wind direction; I am not speaking of one's immediate area, but of travelling to ground thirty miles from home and on

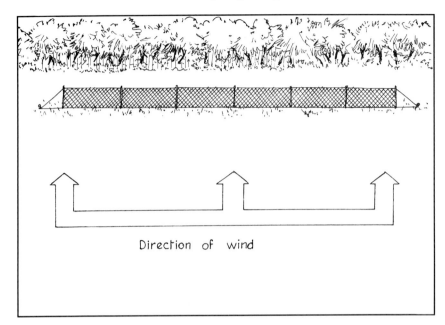

Setting with the wind blowing in this direction is referred to as a plumper.

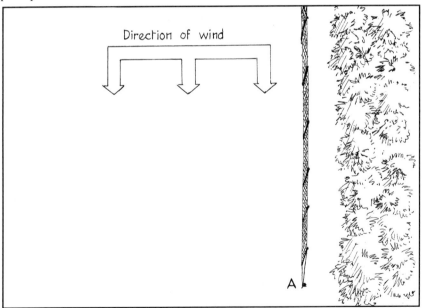

The setting of the wind that blows down the side of the wood is referred to as the end set. The end set should be approached from point A.

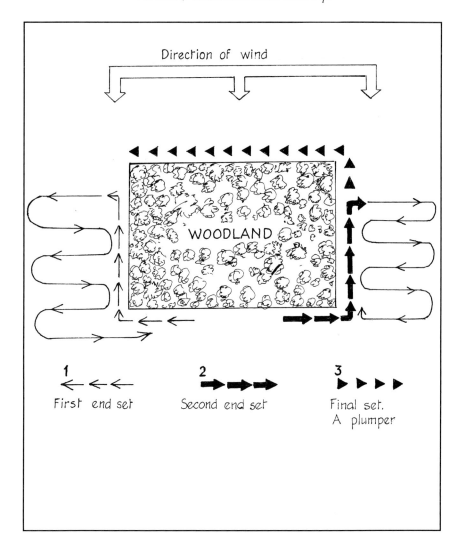

Direction of wind

WOODLAND

1
First end set

2
Second end set

3
Final set.
A plumper

The correct way to work a block of woodland. The first two of the three sets are end sets so it is important not to run the nets the full length of the wood. To do so would ruin the final set which is a plumper. When end setting a block of woodland in this way one should set as far along the wood as indicated then bant the sets as shown. The banting should be silent for the end sets and then the final set should be sound banted.

occasions a good deal further. Alternative number one – on a breezy day, the long netter should phone for the weather forecast for the area he intends to work (the local newspaper will of course give the same information). We shall assume the forecast for that day is a southerly breeze. Off one goes to the ground in question and on arrival walks the side of the wood where the wind strikes, and there is the south; obviously north will strike one's back, west will strike one's right cheek and east the left.

This method will prove successful, but what if the wind drops on arrival at the setting ground as is sometimes the case – do we wait until the sun goes down in the western sky and take a reading from that? No my friend, I travel to the ground in the sure knowledge that on leaving I will have acquired the information as to which wind is necessary to set a particular side of the woodland, or whatever cover I intend to set, but the weather forecast is always checked before leaving home, just to make sure the wind will very likely blow consistently in one direction for the duration of the night. Of course, should the forecast be for a change of wind direction in the early hours of the morning, I alter my plans accordingly.

When long netting before the Second World War, I never bothered with telephone or forecasts, often taking my readings from smoke that belched from nearby factory chimney stacks. I will not continue to bore you with talk of various methods of wind prediction, but in my opinion, the compass takes some beating.

THE DRIPPING FOG

The only conditions under which the long netter may expect to kill large numbers of rabbits when there is little or no wind is on the night of a 'dripping fog'. Even the most uninformed is aware that fog deadens sound; add to that a slight drizzle and the rabbits' handicap becomes insurmountable, as the rain keeps the creatures' ears down.

It was on just such a night, as I waited by the old church gate for the man with whom I had agreed to partner that night, lost in a reverie in which my old friend and partner, Thomas Moor, figured prominently, I was startled out of my musing as a figure materialized out of the encircling grey shroud that was fog. 'Let's go, Harold,' said Jack Ginger. Around six feet was Jack, ruddy complexion and an engaging personality was manifest in his smiling blue eyes. I cast a surreptitious glance at his face as he lit his pipe and the triumphant gleam in his eyes spoke volumes. 'We have got them tonight, kid,' he said, referring to the rabbits' chance of survival under the prevailing conditions.

He was a difficult character to assess, for it was only on rare occasions one saw him unaccompanied by his brother 'Big Dewi'. They made an extremely formidable duo, Jack supplying a considerable amount of shrewd intellect, while Dewi turned the scales at close to seventeen stone, mostly muscle. 'I suppose it's the narrow sets tonight,' said my companion. 'Where else, Jack' was my reply. 'Let's get on with it then,' he grumbled, 'a little colder and it would be a freezing fog.' The fields we were about to net were known to the fraternity as the 'narrow sets' because they were just that. Added to the handicap of the construction of these sets, where the rabbits chose to feed was a further impediment – the lights from a nearby village proved to be a problem of the first magnitude. In fact, this night of the dripping fog was the only occasion when the problem could be solved.

The routine was similar to that worked on any other night, except that there was no bellying up of the rabbits along the foot lines following their chinning, for on such a night as that we were compelled to work by touch alone. Because of this, after chinning, we doubled back along the nets extricating and legging the catch on to slings as we went. The entire catch was left at an anchor pin while the nets were picked up back towards the rabbits, to be picked up prior to moving to another set. Jack Ginger and I did very well that night and made our way homeward quite pleased with our efforts and the results.

It must be remembered that working long nets under these conditions is the most difficult of all, and I would not advise any inexperienced youngsters to set on a dripping fog. The two netters need to know their ground intimately, for when venturing on to unknown territory, it is quite easy to lose one's bearings. The position of every hedge, ditch, gate and tree must be before one's eyes constantly. These various landmarks will enable the netters to retain their sense of direction as they

81

range to and fro across silent fog-bound country.

GUTTING THE CATCH

One may not be too clear as to the manner in which a skilled long netter cleans out his catch, to most people this is known as gutting. I am not talking about gutting in daylight, but by feel alone, and in total darkness if necessary, or for those who prefer it, by the light of a small torch.

In the early warm months of the season, failure to carry out the gutting process may render part of the catch unfit for sale. The removal of the creature's entrails calls for a little care. One should take hold of the pelt on the rabbit's back, clench the hand in order to stretch the belly skin tight, then using a sharp instrument make a small incision of about one inch in the stomach wall. Insert the index finger of each hand and tear open the skin down towards the vent, open the stomach towards the ground and the entrails will fall out. For the purpose of disembowelling, a pair of thin rubber washing-up gloves can be used to protect the hands from the inevitable mess. The drawing of the cutting instrument down the entire length of the stomach tends to cause the bursting of the intestines and often the stomach. Another reason for carrying out this manoeuvre in the field is to reduce the weight of an already heavy burden, especially in the event of having to convey a large catch over any considerable distance.

EARLY AND LATE FEEDING SITES

A further piece of advice mainly for the novice is that of how to be able to tell whether the sets one is about to work are early or late feeding areas. The ability of knowing the time to set a particular stretch of cover in order to make a worth-while catch has its merits. Due to the geography of some estates, there will be the odd set that renders poor returns. Various reasons may be given as the cause. Certain unfamiliar noises may cause the rabbits to feed close to the covert.

It was Thomas Moor, as usual, who enlightened me as to the fact that the problem was of nature's making and easily solved. It was a small set and on the two occasions I had set it my reward

82

was meagre. I explained the problem to Thomas and he offered to accompany me, as I had been working solo for a couple of weeks. On this occasion we set the ground at an hour suggested by the old master, four-thirty in the morning. It was extremely dark and a fresh southerly wind was blowing as we climbed the gate on to the set. Silently we dropped the nets, then got well out and banted back toward them. Not a single scream greeted our approach, causing me to jump to the conclusion that this, like my two previous visits, was a fruitless one, but as I quickly felt my way along the net I encountered, within ten yards, the first of thirteen thrashing bunnies in my two nets.

After picking up and legging the kill onto slings, I found Thomas, who had had similar results. He had long since concluded his task and was sitting on the stump of a tree mid-way along the set. 'Harold,' he said, 'feel the bellies of these rabbits.' I complied with the request and sure enough they felt blown-up and hard. Thomas continued 'You see Harold, the mystery is solved. Their stomachs are full, they are late feeders on this set. I guessed as much when you first explained the situation. Had you felt the bellies of the odd ones you killed on your earlier setting, you would have found the bellies slack and less distended than these, which meant the rabbits had not begun serious feeding when your erstwhile endeavour took place.' Over the years that followed I found his observations to be correct. Once again I had learned something from him, in that instance to differentiate between early and late feeding sets.

OVER-LAMPING

Finally, for netters who also use lamp and dog. it is important not to visit the netting ground for repeated nights of lamping with lurchers, prior to setting with long nets. Over-lamping of sets will quickly trick them and, with the rabbits' reluctance to travel, netting will be a waste of time. If I were a lamper, my first priority would be to remove the main bulk of bunnies with long nets. Then, if so inclined, follow up with a couple of nights lamping.

—7—

Moonlight Ferreting

T HE PRACTICE OF taking rabbits by the light of a full moon, by employing the services of white ferrets, and working them in conjunction with two or more fifty-yard long nets, is an ancient one, used originally, no doubt, by the rabbit poachers of centuries long since past who, being driven by circumstances, not to mention starvation, risked mutilation and even death, to feed their hungry offspring.

Many years ago I myself was a great lover of moonlight ferreting, but of course I had full authority from the landowner in question to go about my business. To give you a clear insight into the art of moonlight ferreting, I think it best that I describe it to you in the following narrative.

Once Upon A Moonlit Night

My companion and I stood gazing south of Wrexham in the direction of the rolling hills of North Shropshire. The road we intended to take was a ribbon of moonlight and the thought came unbidden of that wonderful poem, 'The Highwayman'. My companion was Harry Lavalle, a long netter of no mean ability and a true son of the celtic family, the Welsh branch that is; short, rather stocky and with powerful shoulders, his skin pale, as one might expect of a person hewing coal in the earth's bowels, and the blue scars bearing mute testimony to the blows taken in accidents underground. 'Harry,' I said, 'it was nights such as this that made the Lincolnshire poacher famous,' for according to the song, he must have been a ferreting man, because the long netter cannot function on a clear, frosty moonlight night. 'You're right, Harold,' said my companion.

Strangely enough, one of the marches past of the Welsh Regiment is 'March Past the Lincolnshire Poacher' and it was of interest to us to know that the 69th South Lincolnshire Regiment became the Welsh Regiment, famous as 'The Fighting 69th.' Without more ado we put the ferret bags and nets in my old Austin England and made off down the road that was glistening and sparkling like diamonds in the frosty air, and Harry sang at the top of his voice – 'Oh, 'tis my delight on a shiny night in a season of the year.'

Taking rabbits with ferrets and long nets.

Arriving at our destination at about midnight and after parking the car, we left the road and were soon crossing the frost covered fields and the crunching sound of our marching feet was carried on the still, frosty night air. As a consequence the dogs from nearby farms sounded their warnings, a sure sign that something, or someone, was abroad.

Reaching our first target, an open field warren of fifty holes, we encircled it with our hemp nets, linking them in the correct manner, as this both saves on the use of pegs and ensures no opening is left to facilitate the escape of one or more rabbits. The intermittent barking of the farmyard dogs had long since ceased, lost in the distance and semi-darkness of this frosty January night. Harry introduced three ferrets into the warren, then for an hour we waited for the action to begin.

Hopes of a good result for the night's work were dwindling fast when suddenly the haunting chimes of the village church bell broke the startled air and, with almost eye-baffling speed, two furry forms raced across the warren, struck the net and were instantly dispatched by Harry. A short period of inactivity passed, then my companion 'clicked', sounding the signal used when danger threatened, but on this occasion I knew the warning signified he had heard our quarry racing below ground, being relentlessly pursued by the ferrets. Almost instantly the real action began. Bolting from the warren in twos and threes, the terrified rabbits struck the encircling nets from all directions. The warren had obviously not been worked for some considerable time. Any ferreter will acknowledge that by late season rabbits are quite educated, due to the fact that the warrens have been persistently ferreted during the early months of the season.

By the time the sonorous notes of the church bell drifted down to us through the silvery twilight, tolling the hour of three, twenty-eight rabbits had been enmeshed in the nets, dispatched and extracted to lie belly up along the footline, thereafter to be legged on to two separate slings. By this time the three little warriors had surfaced, each Jill to be returned to her separate bag. Now came the final chore of picking up the nets. Harry and I picked up our own, pegs also. Some less-experienced long netters pick up each net in turn between them, the correct way entails the pegger leading the way when

87

picking up, the reverse being the case when running out.

Having returned the nets to our large poacher's pockets, we moved on to our second and final warren situated along a hawthorn hedge and comprising some twenty holes. Most of these were dug into the hedgerow, but three were pop holes situated about fifteen yards or so from the hedge and scarcely the diameter of a tennis ball. Detection was difficult especially when surrounded by tufts of grass. One had to be diligent in searching for these pop holes, as to miss one was certain to result in the loss of rabbits. On this occasion they were well inside the encircling nets and after one hour the ferrets had bolted fourteen, then surfaced; this indicated that the warren had now been evacuated completely by its occupants.

The importance of linking the nets correctly through the hedge cannot be too strongly emphasised, for there are occasions when the rabbit will emerge from a hedge burrow and run along the inside of the hedge in order to escape. The linked nets will foil this stratagem. However, we had been fairly successful on this wonderful moonlit night and our cup of fun was full and running over. Collecting all our gear we legged the fourteen rabbits on to a sling and on the return journey to the van recovered the other twenty-eight from the low branch of a tree where we hung them to prevent night predators from despoiling them.

Arriving home safely I crept into the bedroom to receive my usual greeting 'Keep those cold feet off me' and I knew failure to observe the command could cause a major upset.

In closing I will give a few final tips on the subject of moonlight ferreting. One often finds rabbits reluctant to flee the warren when snow has fallen; this problem is minimal when day-time ferreting, or on the occasion of a dreaded north-easterly wind. A mild moonlight night can be fairly profitable but for obvious reasons the burrows will not be fully occupied. Finally always make sure the ferrets wear 'belled' collars, for the little creatures, if of the albino or greyhound type, will, on emergence from underground, be indistinguishable from frost or snow; but one is soon alerted by the merry tinkling of the bells as the ferrets shake themselves on emergence.

—8—

The Twilight Years

T IME IS PASSING, and I have considerably passed the allotted span of three score years and ten, shorter in wind and stiffer in limb than of yore. I have reluctantly become semi-retired from what to me was 'The Great Game' and often my thoughts turn to the observation of that great poet Robert Burns, 'If only we could see ourselves as other people see us' – or words to that effect.

In years long since I was seen to be bull-throated with thick powerful arms and broad across the back and shoulders, with strong sturdy legs that served me well over many a year, and hard times along the way. Now I see myself as a shadow, nay, a caricature of the picture drawn. The powerful physique has deteriorated and gauntness of face and dimness of eye bear witness to the encroaching years.

I do not resent growing old, for many are denied that privilege, but the handicap of this old frame does frustrate me at times, especially as I am no longer able to pull my weight when out with the nets. Thank the Lord I am still able to get abroad on windy nights and I am even more grateful that I am blessed with a son who loves the long netting game every bit as much as I do. My lad and I still tread the same sets I first trod fifty and more years ago with Thomas Moor.

It's a strange sensation I receive at times, treading in those same footsteps. Occasionally on the breeze in fancy's piercing sounds I hear old Thomas whispering, 'We will double bant this set, Harold,' or 'Run out the bant, H,' as he sometimes called me. Then at a turn in the wood, when the wind strikes the back and brushes the cheek on the field side of the wood, I sometimes hear that unique jargon of his, 'Let's ride this breeze and drop a back set.' No doubt in a very few years my son will hear the same whisper on the breeze, only then, the whisper will be mine.

Before bringing this book based on a lifetime's long netting to a close, I leave the reader with one final piece of advice. If, in the Autumn, as one treads cautiously and silently along a covert side, intent on dropping one's nets, but fails to hear any rustle of the leaves, there is no point in bothering to set the nets, because the task will prove a fruitless one. Very likely one will hear on these occasions the stamp of the rabbits' feet along the covert side as they become aware of the cautious approach.

Remember this – the long netter's ally is the Wind.